HISTORY'S FAMOUS FEUDS

The Founding Fathers and King George III

Rivals of Colonial America

Lindsey Lowe

Enslow PUBLISHING

Published in 2024 by Enslow Publishing, LLC
2544 Clinton Street
Buffalo, NY 14224

Portions of this work were originally authored by Ellis Roxburgh and
published as *The Founding Fathers vs. King George III: The Fight for a New Nation.*
All new material this edition authored by Lindsey Lowe.

Children's Publisher: Anne O'Daly
Design Manager: Keith Davis
Picture Manager: Sophie Mortimer

Manufactured in the United States of America

CPSIA compliance information: Batch #CSENS24: For further information contact
Enslow Publishing LLC, New York, New York at 1-800-398-2504.

Please visit our website, www.enslowpublishing.com. For a free color catalog of all our high-quality books,
call toll free 1-800-398-2504 or fax 1-877-980-4454.

Cataloging-in-Publication Data

Names: Lowe, Lindsey.
Title: The Founding Fathers and King George III: rivals of colonial America / Lindsey Lowe.
Description: New York : Enslow Publishing, 2024. | Series: History's famous feuds | Includes index.
Identifiers: ISBN 9781978536593 (pbk.) | ISBN 9781978536609 (library bound) | ISBN 9781978536616 (ebook)
Subjects: LCSH: United States--History--Revolution, 1775-1783--Causes--Juvenile literature. |
United States--History--Revolution, 1775-1783--Juvenile literature.
Classification: LCC E210.O34 2024 | DDC 973.3'11--dc23

Front Cover: Library of Congress: top; Art Gallery of South Australia: Allan Ramsay bottom.

Art Gallery of South Australia: Allan Ramsay 1r, 5, 11-19tr, 23-31tr, 25-41tr, 43; HMSO: 9; Library of Congress: 1l,
4, 10, 10-18tl, 11, 20, 22, 22-30tl, 25, 26, 28, 36, 38-40tl, 42; Massachusetts Historical Society: 18; Metropolitan
Museum of Art: 31; National Portrait Gallery: 16, 17; Robert Hunt Library: 6, 7, 8, 14, 15, 19, 30, 38, 39, 45;
Royal Collection: 12, 13; Shutterstock: Tony Spuria 24, Orhan Cam 40, David W. Leindecker 41, 42/43;
Thinkstock: iStock 21, 27; U.S. Architect of the Capitol: 29, 33, 35; U.S. Army Center of Military History 32, 34;
Whitehouse Historical Association: 37; Yale Center for British Art: 23.

t=top, b=bottom, l=left, r=right

Artistic Effects
Shutterstock

Find us on

Contents

Facing Off

The Founding Fathers V King George III

The Founding Fathers were drawn from men across all thirteen colonies. After two decades under British rule, they decided that the colonies should be independent.

- Colonial leaders such as John Adams, Samuel Adams, Benjamin Franklin, and Thomas Jefferson were inspired to react against what they saw as unfair British laws.
- Some of the Founding Fathers hoped they could get George III to rule the colonies in a fairer way.
- When the king refused to make changes, the colonists decided they would be better off governing themselves.

When George III became king in 1760, the American colonies were the most successful of Britain's overseas possessions. But George III and his government did not want to give them the freedoms they wanted.

- George III had a key role in governing Britain and its colonies, with Parliament enforcing his policies.
- George believed that his position as monarch entitled him to treat his subjects—including those in America—as he wished.
- The British government only allowed the American colonies to trade with other British colonies.
- During the French and Indian War (1754–1763), many Americans fought on the side of Britain against the French and their Native American allies. George III upset the colonies by imposing new taxes on them to raise money to pay for the war.

Background

The Seven Years' War ended in 1763. It was a British victory over the French. But the results of this great victory led to the American Revolution.

WAR: George Washington (on horse) fights with the British in the French and Indian War.

Colonial Americans fought alongside Britain in the North American part of the Seven Years' War. This part was known as the French and Indian War (1754–1763). The French were finally driven out of their colony in what is now Canada, which then came under direct British rule.

By 1763, most Americans felt that their loyalty to their colony was more important than their loyalty to Great Britain and the British king. Most colonists had never been to Britain. They found the British soldiers who

"The Sugar Act set people a-thinking, in six months, more than they had done in their whole lives before."

James Otis, 1764

came to North America to fight in the war rude and superior. The soldiers looked down on the colonists, and called them names such as "riffraff" and "Yankees." That suggested that the British did not think much of their American cousins.

Land and Money

Tension grew between the Americans and the British. Although the French had been defeated, their former Native American allies still resisted British rule. To try to keep the Native Americans happy, the British passed a law that was designed to ban colonists from

SUGAR: Barrels of molasses are shipped from Britain's colonies in the Caribbean to America.

> “Taxation without representation is tyranny.”
>
> **James Otis, 1761**

settling west of the Appalachian Mountains. The colonial Americans were furious. The colonies were starting to feel overcrowded and many settlers wanted to move west. The British sent 10,000 troops to help prevent unrest among the Americans. It soon became clear, however, that the British expected the Americans to help pay for the new troops—and for the highly expensive French and Indian War.

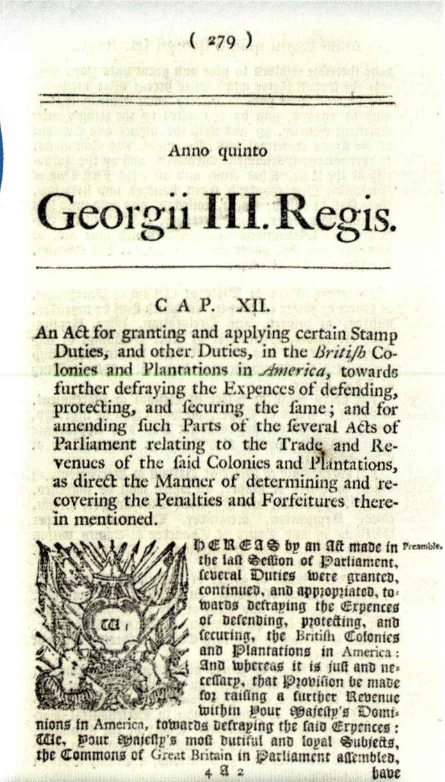

(279)

Anno quinto

Georgii III. Regis.

CAP. XII.

An Act for granting and applying certain Stamp Duties, and other Duties, in the *Britiſh* Colonies and Plantations in *America*, towards further defraying the Expences of defending, protecting, and ſecuring the ſame; and for amending ſuch Parts of the ſeveral Acts of Parliament relating to the Trade and Revenues of the ſaid Colonies and Plantations, as direct the Manner of determining and recovering the Penalties and Forfeitures therein mentioned.

WHEREAS by an Act made in the laſt Seſſion of Parliament, ſeveral Duties were granted, continued, and appropriated, towards defraying the Expences of defending, protecting, and ſecuring, the Britiſh Colonies and Plantations in America: And whereas it is juſt and neceſſary, that Proviſion be made for raiſing a further Revenue within Your Majeſty's Dominions in America, towards defraying the ſaid Expences: We, Your Majeſty's moſt dutiful and loyal Subjects, the Commons of Great Britain in Parliament aſſembled, Preamble.

4 A 2 have

ACT: The Stamp Act of 1765 was the last straw for many Americans.

New Taxes

The British people were against any rise in their taxes. Instead, Prime Minister George Grenville asked the British Parliament to pass the Sugar Act, or Revenue Act, to impose more taxes on the American colonies. The act forced American merchants to pay higher duty on imported molasses. It also meant that most American exports could only be sold to Britain. The terms of the act infuriated colonial Americans.

In 1764, the British introduced the Currency Act. It stopped the colonies issuing their own money. Americans started to form groups to oppose the tightening of British rule. A "committee of correspondence" was formed in Boston to organize support against unpopular laws. In 1764, colonial Americans formed the First Continental Congress, a body intended to represent their opinions. The Congress had no power. The British ignored the colonists' protests and continued to pass legislation that was unpopular.

The Stamp Act

In 1765, the Stamp Act placed a tax on all printed material used in the colonies, from newspapers to playing cards. Colonial Americans felt the British government was interfering too much in their lives. Colonial Americans had no members in the British Parliament, where the new taxes were debated. They could not argue against them. Therefore, they claimed, they should not have to pay them.

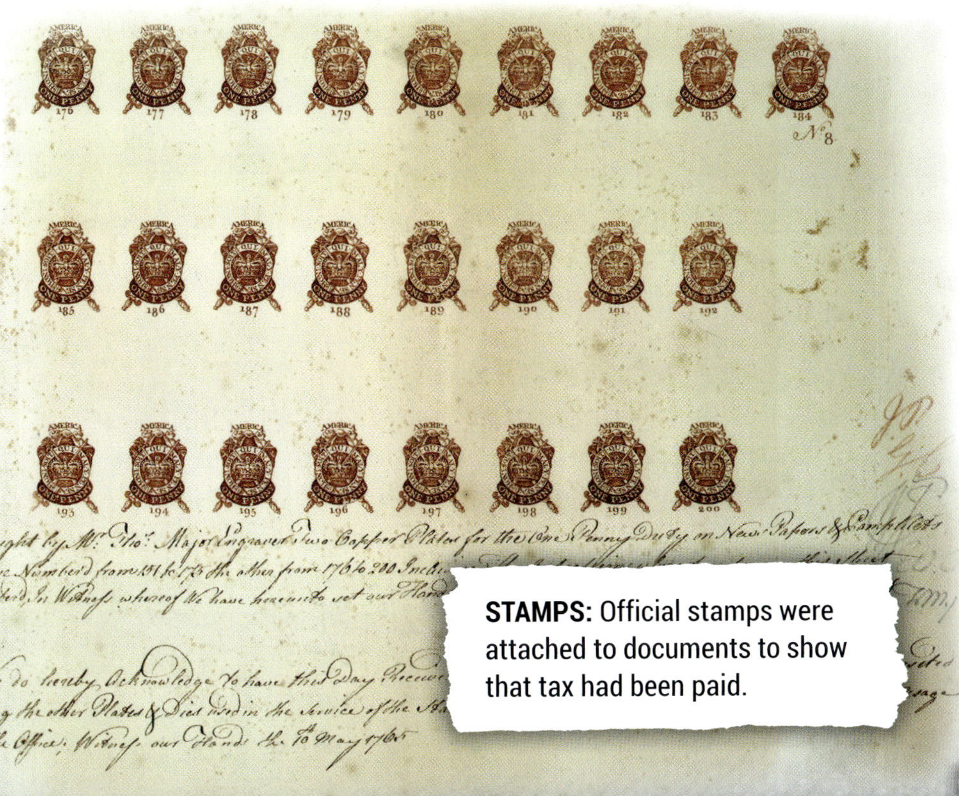

STAMPS: Official stamps were attached to documents to show that tax had been paid.

Founding Fathers

» MEN SHAPING THE NEW COUNTRY

Men from different colonies united to rebel against British rule. They were determined to end its tyranny.

Samuel Adams (1722–1803) was a brewer who formed a group in Boston in 1765 to protest against the hated Stamp Act. His cousin, John Adams (1735–1826), trained as a lawyer and was a prominent figure in Boston. Well educated, he was an early supporter of American independence from Great Britain. Another Bostonian, the wealthy merchant John Hancock (1737–1793), organized protests and was condemned by the British as a "rabble-rouser," or troublemaker.

LEADER: Samuel Adams called on colonial Americans to resist British rule.

Men from Virginia

Further south, Patrick Henry (1736–1799), a Virginian plantation owner, attorney, and politician, condemned the British in the Virginia House of Burgesses. Another Virginian plantation owner, Thomas Jefferson (1743–1826), became a leader of anti-British opinions. Such views came to be described as patriotic. He would later be the main author of the Declaration of Independence.

Benjamin Franklin

The coauthors of the declaration were John Adams and the Philadelphian Benjamin Franklin (1706–1790). Franklin was a writer, scientist, and thinker. He spent time living in Britain, where he negotiated with the government about the colonists' grievances. He was later the American ambassador to France. He was important in getting the French to recognize the United States as a new country. Because of his hard work, Franklin is often called "the first American."

"I repeat it... ...we must fight! An appeal to arms... ...is all that is left to us."

Patrick Henry, March 23, 1775

HANCOCK: John Hancock would become the chairman of the Continental Congress in 1775.

King George III

» THE RULER WHO LOST THE COLONIES

George III wanted to be remembered as a fair ruler. However, taxes imposed on the American colonies led to revolution.

PORTRAIT: This portrait of George III was painted in 1771.

In Britain, King George was popular. Victory over France in the Seven Years' War in 1763 made Great Britain the most powerful nation in the world. George now ruled over new territory in Canada as well as the American colonies and growing areas of Africa, Australia, and India. But the British struggled to pay for this expansion of the empire. The king wanted to be involved in the daily running of the empire, but had no practical experience. He relied on a series of unsuitable prime ministers to guide him, but their influence only made a bad situation worse.

Colonies in Revolt

When the American colonies first protested against his laws and then revolted, George III was furious. He was determined to make the colonists pay for starting a war. When they declared their wish to become independent in 1776, the king

"I am still hoping that my people in America would have discerned the traitorous views of their leaders."

King George III, October 27, 1775

wanted to punish them for their disrespect. He insisted that the war continue even after British victory became unlikely. It was only with defeat in the Battle of Yorktown in 1781 that he accepted the colonists had won and he had lost America.

The struggle over the American colonies would take its toll on George's health. He began to suffer from episodes of mental illness. The episodes grew worse later in his life.

FAMILY: George and his queen, Charlotte, were popular with the British people.

Ideas and Leaders

» THE CASE FOR INDEPENDENCE

Thinkers inspired the Founding Fathers to seek independence. But the Revolutionary War had to be won on the battlefield.

COMMANDER: George Washington led the Continental Army to victory.

Thomas Paine (1737–1809) was a British excise officer who met with Benjamin Franklin in London in 1774. Franklin convinced Paine to sail to America, where he arrived in November, just as the debate about independence was heating up. Paine wrote a pamphlet titled *Common Sense*. He said that the American colonies should become independent as a democracy rather than a monarchy. Paine's pamphlet was an inspiration to many of the Founding Fathers. The Englishman was dubbed "The Father of the American Revolution."

Military Commanders

Few of the Founding Fathers actually fought against Britain, but the generals who led the Continental Army were key to the success of the Revolution. George Washington (1732–1799) was the commander in chief of the newly created army. He would become America's first president after independence. Nathanael Greene (1742–1786)

IDEAS: In *Common Sense*, Thomas Paine laid out the case for the revolution.

served as a major general in the Continental Army, as did the French-born Marquis de Lafayette (1757–1834). Lafayette was so impressed by the principles behind the American Revolution that he took them back to France, which had its own revolution in 1789.

Benedict Arnold

Benedict Arnold was a Patriot commander until 1780, when he grew angry at not being promoted and switched sides. When the Americans tried to arrest him, he fled and served as a general in the British army for the rest of the war.

> "The cause of America is in a great measure the cause of all mankind."
>
> **Thomas Paine, Common Sense, 1776**

The King's Advisors

» THE MEN BEHIND GEORGE III

The men George III chose to be his advisors proved to have poor judgment. They failed to give good advice.

The Earl of Bute was an ambitious Scottish nobleman. He had been the king's tutor when George was a young boy. When he came to the throne in 1760, George made the earl his secretary of state. Two years later, the earl became prime minister. Bute was deeply unpopular—partly because he was Scottish, which the English resented—and only served 11 months in office. He helped end the political control of the nonconformist Whig party that had dominated British politics.

NORTH: Lord North wanted to defeat American protests by military force.

Lord North

George's next choice of prime minister was even worse. Lord Frederick North held the office for 12 disastrous years. North was a favorite of the king, who persuaded him to form a government in 1770. North believed the unrest in the colonies would lead to calls for American independence. He led Britain to war against its colonies. North's strategic planning led to catastrophic British defeats at Saratoga in 1777 and Yorktown in 1781.

With the war going badly, North wanted to resign, but George III would not let him. North had to stay in his post until the war was over.

William Pitt the Elder

Many British politicians opposed the war. They included the former prime minister, William Pitt the Elder. He said he understood the Americans' anger. He wanted the war to be ended quickly, even if it meant giving in to American demands.

OPPOSITION: William Pitt was called the Elder to distinguish him from his son, Pitt the Younger, who later also became prime minister.

> "While a foreign troop was landed in my country, I never would lay down my arms. Never! Never! Never!"
>
> **William Pitt the Elder, 1777**

Taking a Stand

» THE COLONISTS COME TOGETHER

In response to the Stamp Act of 1765, the American colonists started to organize themselves into a united front.

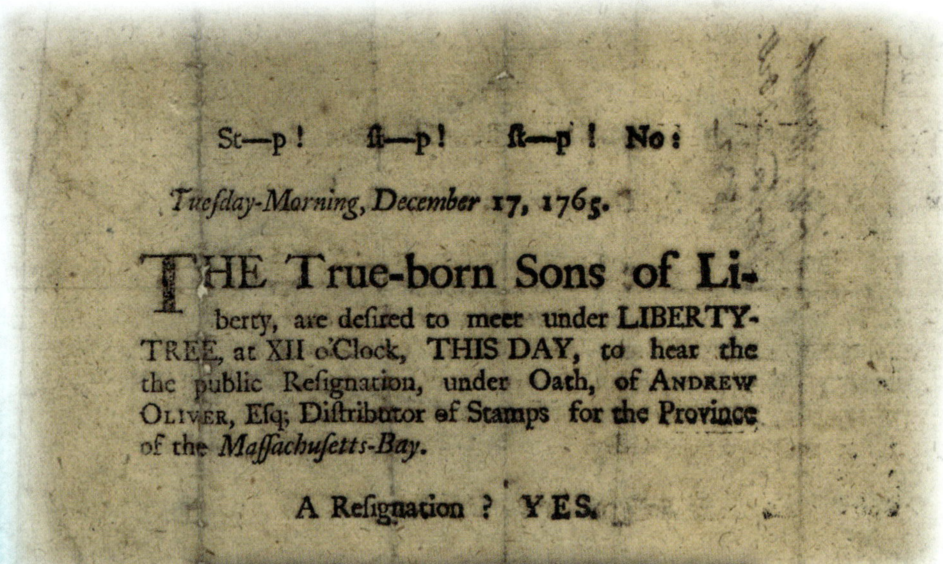

St—p! ſt—p! ſt—p! No:

Tueſday-Morning, *December* 17, 1765.

THE True-born Sons of Liberty, are deſired to meet under LIBERTY-TREE, at XII o'Clock, THIS DAY, to hear the the public Reſignation, under Oath, of ANDREW OLIVER, Eſq; Diſtributor of Stamps for the Province of the *Maſſachuſetts-Bay*.

A Reſignation ? YES.

NOTICE: This note asks the Sons of Liberty to protest against a British official.

Representatives of nine colonies met in 1765 at the Stamp Act Congress. They wrote to the British government to say they would not pay taxes unless they were ordered to by their own colonial representatives. Other Americans formed groups such as the Sons of Liberty, which urged people not to buy British goods. A women's group called the Daughters of Liberty wove their own cloth so that they did not need to buy British cloth.

> “Our country is in danger, but not to be despaired of. Our enemies are numerous and powerful; but we have many friends, determining to be free, and heaven and earth will aid the resolution.”

Joseph Warren, Boston Massacre Oration, 1772

The Boston Massacre

George III was outraged, but the boycott damaged British trade, so the Stamp Act was repealed in 1766. However, the next year, the British introduced more taxes. Tensions in the colonies were high. On March 5, 1770, a group of Bostonians threw snowballs at some British soldiers. A crowd gathered, and the British opened fire, killing five civilians in what became known as

MASSACRE: British troops open fire on protesters in Boston in March 1770.

SUPPORT: Bostonians encourage protesters heading for the British tea ships.

> "No man should hesitate to use arms in defense of so valuable a blessing. Yet arms should be the last resort."
>
> **George Washington, August 27, 1776**

the Boston Massacre. Later, no one could say which side had fired the first shot.

Army of Civilians

To avoid further confrontation, the governor, Thomas Hutchinson, pulled the British troops out of Boston. Meanwhile the colonists of Massachusetts set up more "committees of correspondence" to organize local resistance to the British authorities. Many volunteers also signed up as minutemen. These members of the colonial militia got their name from the fact they were said to be ready to fight at a minute's notice.

The Boston Tea Party

In 1773, the British parliament passed the Tea Act, giving British traders a monopoly on importing tea to the colonies. In Boston, around 5,000 "Patriots" met on December 16, 1773, to protest against the act. Around 50 men boarded British tea ships in Boston Harbor. They dressed as Native Americans to underline the fact that this was an American protest. They threw 342 chests of tea overboard. George III ordered the closure of Boston port, the most important port in New England. The king's order showed that he was determined to put a stop to American protests.

MINUTEMEN: The best members of the militia became minutemen, who were ready to fight at a moment's notice.

Intolerable Acts

FLASHPOINT » HARSH NEW LAWS

George III was outraged by the Boston Tea Party. In response, his government imposed further taxes on the American colonists.

OCCUPIED: British troops had been in Boston since they first arrived in 1768.

The British closed the port of Boston. In the spring of 1774, George III also ordered parliament to pass a series of laws the Americans called "the Intolerable Acts." These limited town meetings to just one a year. They also allowed officials working for the British who were accused of breaking the law in America to be tried in Britain. The acts allowed British soldiers to force colonists to give them food and lodging in their homes. In addition, the unpopular commander in chief of British forces, Thomas Gage, was made governor of Massachusetts. The colony was now effectively under military rule.

George III believed he had done enough to snuff out any rebellion. On June 22, 1774, he signed a new law to extend the boundaries of French-speaking Quebec in Canada. The king's tolerance toward the Catholic French Canadians infuriated Protestant Americans.

Dissent

George had dissolved colonial legislatures. Instead, colonies elected unofficial conventions. Militiamen ignored British orders but attended secret drill sessions organized by local Patriot committees. More significantly, many colonists refused to pay their taxes to British officials and instead paid them to Patriot taxmen.

> "They will be lions, whilst we are lambs, but if we take the resolute part they will undoubtedly prove very meek."
>
> **George III to Lord North, 1774**

UNPOPULAR: Thomas Gage was an unpopular governor of Massachusetts.

Continental Congress

FLASHPOINT » IMPORTANT DECISIONS

The Intolerable Acts had infuriated the American colonists. They met together to discuss rebellion against the British.

HALL: The Second Continental Congress was held in Independence Hall, Philadelphia.

Representatives from 12 colonies—Georgia did not attend—met at the First Continental Congress in Philadelphia in September 1774. They elected Peyton Randolph as their president. John Adams represented Massachusetts and George Washington attended as a representative of Virginia. The delegates discussed the best way to show George III how much Americans resented his laws. Some thought they should write a letter asking the British government to respect American rights. Others believed the only way to show

George they were serious was to fight. Congress wrote to the king to ask him to repeal the Intolerable Acts and to lift the taxes on the colonies. They also decided to stop buying British goods and to form a militia. This was an army of civilians that could fight in an emergency.

American Opinion Divided

It took weeks for news of the Congress to reach Britain. George III still believed his colonial subjects would not rebel. Few Americans thought about independence. When war came, about one-third of Americans remained loyal to the British crown (Loyalists), while another third wanted independence (Patriots). The final third was undecided. When the Continental Congress met for a second time in May 1775, events had moved on quickly.

> "The dye is now cast, the Colonies must either submit or triumph."
>
> **King George III to Lord North, September 11, 1774**

DEBATE: Representatives at the Congress debated how best to react to Britain's new laws.

The First Shots

FLASHPOINT » LEXINGTON AND CONCORD

The king became more determined to crush American resistance as the Patriots prepared for armed conflict. The first shots were soon fired.

GREEN: Militiamen lie wounded as British troops open fire on Lexington Green.

For many citizens of Massachusetts, war with Great Britain seemed inevitable by early 1775. George III already believed his government had weakened itself by repealing the Stamp Act. He made it clear that he would not give in to the colonies on any other issues.

Patriots in Massachusetts began to stockpile gunpowder and arms in Concord, a town close to Boston. In April 1775, Thomas Gage, the governor of Massachusetts, ordered 700 troops to seize the supplies. Gage ordered them to head to the town of Lexington. He told them to arrest Samuel Adams, John Hancock, and other American leaders. The Patriots soon learned of Gage's plan.

Paul Revere's Midnight Ride

On the night of April 18, 1775, the Patriots Paul Revere, William Dawes, and Samuel Prescott rode from Boston to warn people that the British "redcoats" (soldiers) were coming. When the soldiers arrived in Lexington, 70 militia known as minutemen were waiting. A shot was fired. The war had started. After a brief fight in Lexington, the British won and marched on to Concord. There they met stiff resistance and were forced to retreat all the way to Boston. After the first day of the revolution, 95 Americans and 273 British had lost their lives.

"Don't fire unless fired upon, but if they mean to have a war, let it begin here."

John Parker, Lexington, April 19, 1775

BRIDGE: Much of the fighting at Concord was focused on the town's North Bridge.

The Declaration of Independence

FLASHPOINT » BREAKING WITH BRITAIN

On July 4, 1776, the Declaration of Independence was issued. It was written by three of the Founding Fathers.

WRITING: (left to right) Benjamin Franklin, John Adams, and Thomas Jefferson drafted the Declaration of Independence.

Common Sense, the pamphlet written by the British thinker Thomas Paine, had put into words the grievances many Americans felt against the rule of George III. In the first half of 1776, the booklet sold more than 100,000 copies. Many Americans believed strongly in the creation of a new nation, one not ruled by a royal family. In June 1776, the Second Continental Congress asked a committee to write a Declaration of Independence. Congress made more than 80 further changes, and adopted the declaration on July 4, 1776.

List of Complaints

The declaration was as much a list of complaints as it was a declaration of freedom. Its principal

author, Thomas Jefferson, listed the king's "repeated injuries and usurpations" toward the American people. The declaration argued that the king's poor rule of his colonies meant the Americans should be allowed to govern themselves. What particularly infuriated George III was the document's famous assertion that "All Men are created equal." For centuries, Europeans had been brought up to believe that monarchs were superior to any other human beings.

An Act of Treason

By issuing the declaration, the Founding Fathers risked death for showing disloyalty to the Crown. They were still British, but they were threatening to break away from Britain to form the United States of America. This was a form of treason. But to Americans, the signers offered them the right to life, liberty, and happiness in whatever way they chose.

> "George III is unfit to be the ruler of a free people."
>
> **Declaration of Independence, 1776**

SIGNING: Jefferson and his colleagues present their document to the Congress.

Full-Scale War

FLASHPOINT » FIGHTING THE BRITISH ARMY

The fighting that began in 1775 was the start of a long war. The colonists created a new army to fight experienced British troops.

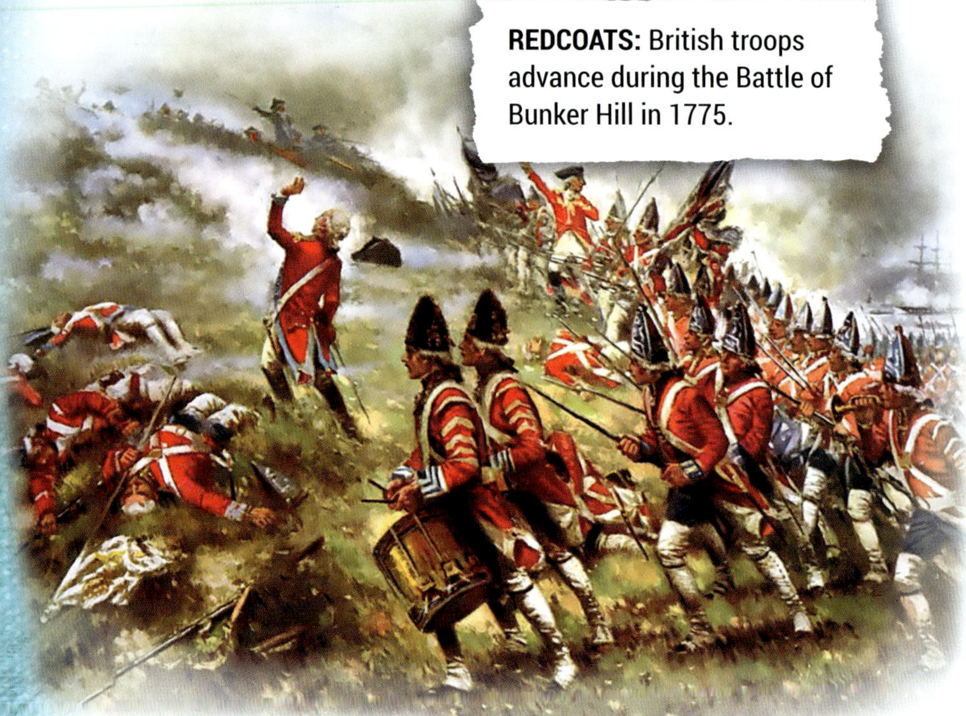

REDCOATS: British troops advance during the Battle of Bunker Hill in 1775.

Congress appointed George Washington to be commander in chief of the newly formed Continental Army. He had to train his militia to fight the British Army, who were known to be the best-trained soldiers in the world. Washington's army was also outnumbered. In August 1776, the Continental Army numbered 18,000. British forces in America at the time, under General William Howe, numbered 41,000 soldiers.

> “You are all marksmen. Don’t one of you fire until you see the whites of their eyes. Then fire low!”
>
> **Israel Putnam, Battle of Bunker Hill, 1775**

The First Year

The British planned to raise troops from among Loyalists. Their support was particularly strong in New York City and in the South. Meanwhile the Americans sent troops north to attack the British in Canada. They were unsuccessful and retreated, followed by a British army that headed south into the colonies.

After the Battles of Lexington and Concord, the British retreated to Boston. They fought the Patriots in the Battle of Bunker Hill and won a costly victory. The Patriots then besieged the British in the port of Boston. Soon afterward, a Patriot army was defeated at New York City.

DELAWARE: George Washington crosses the Delaware River before a surprise attack.

TRENTON: American soldiers capture an enemy cannon in the Battle of Trenton.

The Battle of Saratoga

The Americans scored important victories in December 1776 and January 1777 at Trenton and Princeton, New Jersey. But the tide turned as the British marched south from Canada, winning victories at Fort Ticonderoga, New York, and Bennington, Vermont, in summer 1777. The British supply lines grew too long and hard to maintain, however. That allowed the Continental Army to defeat the British Army from Canada at Saratoga, New York, in October 1777.

> "Our cruel and unrelenting enemy leaves us only the choice of brave resistance, or the most abject submission."
>
> **George Washington, August 27, 1776, before the Battle of Long Island**

Winter at Valley Forge

The victory at Saratoga destroyed British plans, but as winter arrived the Continental Army headed into camp at Valley Forge, Pennsylvania. Nearly one-quarter of the soldiers died from lack of food, the cold, and sickness. But Washington took the opportunity to drill his men. His army became more disciplined.

Help from Europe

In spring 1778 came the news that King George III most feared. France and Spain, traditional enemies of the British, were going to support the Americans by sending troops and money. This was a bitter blow. George believed the French and Indian War had established British power in America. Now his enemies were working with the rebels to overthrow British rule. George refused to give in, however. He argued that giving in would destroy Britain's prosperity, power, and prestige. He believed that, even with foreign help, the rebels would eventually run out of money and back down. He was wrong.

SURRENDER: The British surrender at the Battle of Saratoga, a defeat that led France to enter the war.

Battle of Yorktown

FLASHPOINT » BRITISH FORCES SURRENDER

With French help, the American army surrounded the British at Yorktown. It was to be the last major battle of the war.

ATTACK: American soldiers, in blue, attack the British defenses at Yorktown.

After the battle at Saratoga in 1777, the focus of the fighting moved south to the Carolinas, where there were many Loyalists. The British won a series of battles, but at a heavy price. They were running out of men, supplies, and equipment. Their commander, General Lord Charles Cornwallis, headed for Yorktown at the southern end of

Chesapeake Bay, Virginia, on August 1, 1781, to set up a naval base for an attack on Virginia. The British built defensive works as they waited for reinforcements to arrive by sea. They faced a siege from troops led by George Washington's lieutenant, the Marquis de Lafayette.

British Surrender

French ships arrived before the British reinforcements and blockaded the mouth of Chesapeake Bay. No British ships could get through. Meanwhile Washington marched 7,000 American and French troops from New York to join the siege. Cornwallis and his men were surrounded. He had no hope of receiving any reinforcements. He had no option but to surrender to the Patriots on October 19, 1781. The last battle of the Revolution was over.

"If you cannot relieve me very soon, you must be prepared to hear the worst."

Lord General Cornwallis, September 17, 1781

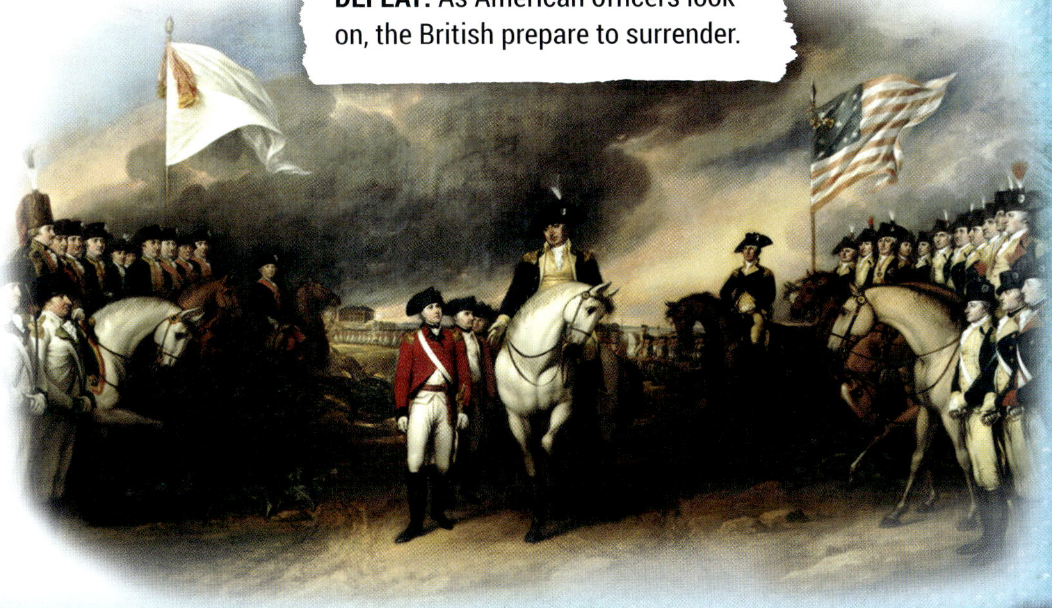

DEFEAT: As American officers look on, the British prepare to surrender.

A New Nation

» CREATING AN INDEPENDENT COUNTRY

After the Founding Fathers won the war against George III they had to decide what kind of nation the United States would be.

CELEBRATION: George Washington rides into New York at the end of the war in 1783.

When John Adams wrote his autobiography at the age of 88, he reflected that the Declaration of Independence had been too personally directed against George III. He said it was "too much like scolding" than being a solemn document.

The Founding Fathers had different opinions of the king. Some tolerated him, but others hated him. Benjamin Franklin and Thomas Jefferson

> "Blows must decide whether they are to be subject to this Country or independent."
>
> **King George III, November 1774**

both blamed the king personally for the harshness of British rule. Even after independence, Jefferson continued to blame George personally for Britain's severe colonial rule. As U.S. ambassador to France, Jefferson met the king in 1786. He said the king was rude to him. In contrast, John Adams, who became the first U.S. ambassador to England, was delighted when he was presented to the King at St. James's Palace in June 1785. He said the king treated him with respect and accepted the independence of his former colony.

The World Stage

Whatever the personal feelings of the Founding Fathers toward the king, it no longer really mattered what they thought of him or what he thought of them. Like Britain, the United States was now recognized around the world as an independent state. They were equals on the world stage and would be expected to behave as such.

PRESIDENT: Thomas Jefferson was elected president in 1801.

End of a Reign

» THE MADNESS OF KING GEORGE

King George III regarded the loss of the colonies as his personal failure. The last years of his reign were troubled.

FUNERAL: King George III died in 1820.

George III never accepted that the colonies had a right to independence. He believed that, as king, he had a divine right to rule Britain's empire. But George's attitude toward the colonies was complex. He believed that the Stamp Act was unfair, but when it was repealed, he felt his government had been too lenient.

As the war progressed, the prime minister, Lord North, repeatedly asked George to negotiate peace. The king refused. Even after defeat at Yorktown, George did not accept defeat. It was only on December 5, 1782, that the king acknowledged American independence.

A Popular King

Defeat in America dented George's popularity at home, but he soon regained it through his frugal lifestyle and devotion to his wife and children. Britain also enjoyed an economic boom while George led European opposition to the rise of Napoleon in France.

By now, however, the King was suffering from episodes of a form of madness. He made his last public speech in October 1810. Growing increasingly sick, George lived the last 10 years of his reign locked away in a hospital while his unpopular son ruled in his place.

> *"Future ages will scarce believe the hardiness of one man... to build a blatant and undisguised tyranny."*
>
> **Thomas Jefferson**

PRINNY: The king's son, Prince George, was called Prinny and was mocked for his extravagant lifestyle.

Aftermath

» PEACE AND ANOTHER WAR

Despite the loss of America, Britain's empire continued to grow. Meanwhile the Founding Fathers had a new country to create.

CAPITAL: The Founding Fathers had a new capital created at Washington, D.C.

As the Founding Fathers argued about the political shape of the new country, George Washington became the first president of the United States of America in 1789 and served until 1797. The young country faced many obstacles, including paying for the war. Congress was given the right to raise taxes, the same problem that had caused the

> We began a contest for liberty ill provided with the means for the war, relying on our patriotism to supply the deficiency.
>
> **George Washington, 1781**

rebellion in the first place. Another problem was what to do with the Loyalists. Many of them moved north to Canada. As for King George III, he argued that he was happy to sacrifice his own desires for those of his colonial subjects.

The War of 1812

There was more trouble to come between Britain and the United States. The War of 1812 broke out over remaining disputes between the two countries. The main cause was trade rights, and Britain's right to search U.S. ships at sea in case they were trading with Britain's enemy, France. British troops burned down large parts of Washington, D.C., the new American capital. The war ended indecisively in 1815. It was the last time the Americans were to fight their former colonial rulers.

LIBERTY: The Liberty Bell in Philadelphia was rung to mark the Declaration of Independence.

Final Judgment

The Founding Fathers V King George III

Which of the rivals came out on top? Although the Founding Fathers had achieved independence, there were still many arguments to be fought over the development of the United States.

- The Founding Fathers established a new country, but argued among themselves about the political shape of the young republic.
- The U.S. Constitution was written in 1789 and is still in force today.
- The Founders were criticized for claiming that "all men were created equal" when some owned slaves.
- In 1861 the country broke apart in civil war, mainly over the issue of slavery.

The subjects of King George III soon forgave him for his loss of the American colonies. However, historians see his rule in a more negative light.

- Historians argue that if George had not been so arrogant toward the American colonies he could have resolved their complaints.
- That would have avoided the American demand for more rights turning into a war for independence.
- The king's mental illness meant that for the last decade of his life his unpopular son, Prince George, ruled in his place.
- Even after it had lost the 13 American colonies, Britain went on to become the world's largest empire in the 19th century, gaining significant territory in Asia and Africa.

Timeline

American complaints about the rule of George III began over a decade before the argument finally flared into a military conflict. The British refused to listen to the colonists' arguments.

1760

A New King
In September, Prince George comes to the throne of the United Kingdom as King George III. He rules colonies around the world, including in North America, India, and Australia.

1763

End of the War
The French and Indian War ends in the defeat of France and its native allies. The British want the American colonies to pay toward the cost of the war.

1765

New Taxes
In March, the British parliament passes a new Stamp Act. It taxes all printed documents in the American colonies. A protest campaign eventually leads to the repeal of the act.

1770

Boston Massacre
In March, British soldiers shoot dead five civilians after Bostonians gather to protest against new taxes placed on the colonies.

1773

Boston Tea Party
In May, Bostonians dressed as Native Americans throw tea from British ships into Boston Harbor to protest against new taxes on tea.

1774

Intolerable Acts
In April, the British begin to pass a series of acts to punish the revolt in Boston, including the Boston Tea Party. The Americans call these measures the "Intolerable Acts."

1774

Continental Congress
In September, representatives from 12 of the 13 colonies gather to discuss a coordinated response to the Intolerable Acts.

1775

First Shots
In April, British redcoats clash with Patriot militia at Lexington and Concord, the first fighting of the Revolutionary War.

1776

Declaration
In July, the Second Continental Congress issues the Declaration of Independence, a list of complaints about why George III is not a fit ruler for the Americans.

1781

Battle of Yorktown
The Revolutionary War comes to an end when the Continental Army and its French allies trap the British army in Virginia and force it to surrender.

1783

Treaty of Paris
In September, the Treaty of Paris formally ends the Revolutionary War and confirms the independence of the United States. The last British troops leave New York.

1789

President
George Washington, former commander of the Continental Army, becomes the first president of the United States.

Glossary

ambassador An official who represents his or her government in a foreign country.

boycott To deliberately stop buying goods from a particular country or manufacturer.

colonists People who live in a colony that is governed by another country.

committee of correspondence A group set up in the American colonies in order to exchange information and help organize resistance against the British.

congress A formal gathering in which delegates discuss important issues.

divine right The right to rule a country, believed to be given to a king or queen by God.

duty A tax charged on imported goods.

legislature An elected body that has the power to make or change laws.

Loyalist A colonial American who remained loyal to Britain during the Revolution.

militia Citizen soldiers who are trained in a similar way to the army.

minutemen Patriot militia who were ready to rush to military service at a moment's notice.

monopoly A situation in which a single company controls the supply of a particular type of goods.

pamphlet A small, thin book with a paper cover.

Patriot Someone who supported the cause of American independence.

plantation A large estate for growing crops such as tobacco or cotton.

redcoat A regular soldier in the British Army.

repeal To reverse a law so it is no longer valid.

revenue Money that is collected by a government through taxes.

strategic Related to a plan to achieve a long-term goal rather than an immediate result.

treason Planning to overthrow the government of one's country.

tyranny Cruel and unfair treatment by people with power, such as government officials.

Further Resources

Books

Berne, Emma Carlson. *The History of the American Revolution*. Rockridge Press, 2021.

Braun, Eric. *The Real Thomas Jefferson: The Truth Behind the Legend.* Capstone Publishing, 2020.

Finch, Fletcher C. *Considering Different Opinions Surrounding the American Revolutionary War.* Rosen Publishing, 2019.

Hesleden, Michael. *Benjamin Franklin, American Diplomat.* Rosen Publishing, 2016.

Lassieur, Allison. *The Real John Adams: The Truth Behind the Legend.* Capstone Publishing, 2020.

Manger, Katherine. *Let's Find Out. Primary Sources. The Declaration of Independence.* Rosen Publishing, 2019.

Raum, Elizabeth, Matt Doeden, Blake Hoena. *You Choose: Founding the United States; Building a New Nation.* Capstone Publishing, 2020.

Websites

www.pbs.org/ktca/liberty/
Extensive interactive website to support the PBS documentary series *Liberty!*

www.history.com/topics/american-revolution
History.com page with many videos about the Revolution.

www.digitalhistory.uh.edu
Click on "American Revolution" to access Digital History's resources for the period.

www.historyplace.com/unitedstates/revolution
Revolutionary War timelines on The History Place website.

Publisher's note to educators and parents: Our editors have carefully reviewed these websites to ensure that they are suitable for students. Many websites change frequently, however, and we cannot guarantee that a site's future contents will continue to meet our high standards of quality and educational value. Be advised that students should be closely supervised whenever they access the Internet.

Index